Whatever Happened to ou
or Taking another look at Chr

Many people feel that Methodism has lost its wa
great blessings which we do enjoy. The faith
phenomenal growth of Easter People, the very
growth in the number of those who want to belc _ ..._ ...yanisation and align
themselves with its emphases; all these are significant indications that God has not deserted the people called Methodists. Yet many of us have, from time to time, the sense that Methodism is no longer a movement within our land. Organisation and structure often replace dynamic and when asked 'What are we here for?' many of our people have difficulty understanding the question, let alone attempting an answer.

I want to contrast the mood of those observations with three quotations from John Wesley. In a letter written to Robert Carr Brackenbury on September 15th 1789 he wrote, 'Full sanctification is the grand depositum which God had lodged with the people called Methodists; and for the sake of propagating this chiefly He appeared to have raised us up.'[1]

Four months before he died he wrote to Adam Clarke, 'If we can prove that any of our Local Preachers or Leaders, either directly or indirectly, speak against it [i.e. Christian Perfection] let him be a Local Preacher or Leader no longer. I doubt whether he shall continue in the Society.'[2]

At the 1763 Conference the question was asked 'What may we reasonably believe to be God's design in raising up the preachers called Methodists?' and the answer was given, 'To reform the nation and, in particular, the Church; to spread scriptural holiness through the land.'[3] We can have no doubt about the significance of the question, and the answer given, when we remember that it was repeated at every Conference for the next twenty-six years. John Wesley was clear about his intention of keeping this central calling of the Methodist people before all his preachers.

Despite all the criticisms and hostility which he faced as he proclaimed the doctrine he remained unmoved. This was the very reason for the existence of the people called Methodists.

Further, he saw the proclamation of the doctrine as the key to church growth; or rather, when societies declined in numbers Wesley knew where to look for the cause. He wrote

> 'One reason is, Christian Perfection has been little insisted on; and whenever this is not done, be the preachers ever so eloquent, there is little increase, either in number or grace of the hearers'[4]

For Wesley Christian Perfection, Entire Sanctification, Perfect Love (call it what you will) was absolutely central. He saw it as nothing less than New Testament Christianity; and God had raised up the Methodist people to call the whole Church

---

[1] John Wesley. The Letters of John Wesley Ed. J. Telford. Epworth, 1931. Vol. 8.238
[2] ibid., p. 249
[3] The Large Minutes, 1862
[4] W.E. Sangster The Path to Perfection London, Hodder & Stoughton. 1943. 26

back to this. Here we are dealing with the core of Methodist faith, and if we have lost this it's no wonder we have lost our way; for this is the reason for our very existence. Before considering Wesley's teaching in some detail we would do well to observe his own personal pilgrimage.

Wesley's Consuming Passion and Quest for Holiness

If the seed of a quest for holiness had been sown in Wesley's heart in the kitchen of the Epworth Rectory it came to fruition during his days at Oxford. Driven again to the writings of Christian classics he had sought that holiness without which no man will see God. The Moravians and the Aldersgate experience had a profound effect, but it is not until later that we begin to see the doctrine of Christian Perfection taking shape. Even then it was not set out as the climax of a systematic theology. It was preached before it was formulated as a doctrinal treatise. One almost feels that the doctrine was so much a part of what Wesley believed a Christian to be that it was set out and proclaimed simply as a statement of what being a Christian involved. In 1742 he produced a tract *The Character of a Methodist* in which he describes a perfect Christian, for this is what he believed a Christian should be. It was when the doctrine was challenged that he found it necessary to formulate a defence which could be used for both enquirers and opponents alike.

It is impossible to separate Wesley's own quest for holiness and the doctrine of Christian Perfection. He felt so strongly about the doctrine because holiness was the passion of his own life. It may help, however, to set down clearly the rational progression in Wesley's thought. Within such a progression we can clearly identify the several elements within what is now popularly called the Wesleyan Quadrilateral - Scripture, Reason, Tradition and Experience. The doctrine is clearly taught in **scripture**. Wesley's own **experience** in searching for holiness is a significant feature. His quest and the subsequent formulation of the doctrine is entirely in keeping with the **tradition** of the Church as expressed in the Christian classics, the collects and Homilies of the Church of England, on which he relied so heavily. And the whole formulation of the doctrine is so logically set forth as to indicate the crucial part which **reason** plays in the whole exercise.

We shall attempt to trace the progress in Wesley's thought;

1. The doctrine centres on the grace of God. It is all of grace. Even the longing for holiness in the heart of man is evidence that God's prevenient grace is in operation. Natural man has no thought for God or the things of God, much less would he make a quest for holiness his own. It is only as a result of God's grace going before man's search that his heart is quickened to the things of God. It is by grace that we are saved. If we are to be sanctified it will be by grace. The provisions which God has made for our growth and development in the Christian life are best described as 'the means of grace'.

2. The scriptures point to the *normal* Christian life as being more than that which was wrought by justification alone i.e. when one becomes a Christian. Reading the picture of the Christian life which is displayed in the scriptures Wesley saw a

HEADLINE SPECIAL

Whatever happened to our Raison D'Etre?

Taking Another Look at Christian Perfection

1997 HEADWAY
METHODIST CONFERENCE
LECTURE

D. PAUL C. SMITH

MOORLEY'S Print & Publishing

© Copyright 1997 HEADWAY

All rights reserved. No part of this publication may be
reproduced, stored in a retrieval system, or
transmitted, in any form or by any means,
electronic, mechanical, photocopying, recording
or otherwise, without the prior
written permission of the Publishers.

ISBN 0 86071 485 3

British Library Cataloguing in Publication Data.
A catalogue record for this book is available
from the British Library.

MOORLEY'S Print & Publishing
23 Park Rd., Ilkeston, Derbys DE7 5DA
Tel/Fax: (0115) 932 0643

contrast and sometimes a contradiction between that picture and the experience of many so-called Christian people. They were living far below the offer and promise of the New Testament.

3. Wesley's logic convinced him that God would not require that for which He did not provide the means. For Wesley the command implies the promise. He would often call such commands 'covered promises'.e.g. If we are commanded to love the Lord our God with all our heart, soul, mind and strength; and our neighbours as ourselves there must be the possibility of fulfilling that requirement. Anything otherwise is contrary to the plain morality of God. An individual Christian who realises that he does not fulfil God's requirements is consequently directed to seek a power which will enable him to do so. The very fact that God requires a certain attitude implies that such an attitude must be possible.

Further, if God requires the fulfilment of the law in this life it is entirely reasonable to expect the power to fulfil God's requirement in this life too. If holiness is what God requires, holiness must be possible. If holiness is what God requires here and now, holiness must be possible here and now.

4. For Wesley the 'Great Salvation' (by which he understood the whole saving work of God) is all by God's grace. Commenting on Jesus' words 'apart from Me you can do nothing' Wesley says,

> In every state we need Christ in the following respects:- (1) Whatever grace we receive, it is a free gift from Him. (2) We receive it as His purchase, merely in consideration of the price He paid. (3) We have this grace, not only from Christ, but in Him.[5]

The idea of any individual gaining God's favour as a result of his actions, attitudes or behaviour is quite alien to Wesley. Our whole salvation is by God's grace alone.

5. Consequently, any holiness or Christian Perfection which the believer may know is the result of God's grace and not or his own endeavour. Wesley, therefore, avoided the heresy of justification by faith and sanctification by works. Through this crucial step in his thinking Wesley established the principle that holiness is itself a gift from God. We are not made holy be what we do, but by what God does in us.

6. Thus, Wesley concluded that both scripture and experience (his own and others) point to a dimension of Christian living which is more profound than that received at justification. It is possible to be justified, and still not experience the kind of Christian living of which the New Testament speaks. A deeper work of grace must be possible. Through it righteousness will be imparted rather than imputed. It will effect a change in our nature rather than just remit the guilt of past sins. It will transport the Christian into the dimension of New Testament holiness.

7. Contrary to popular opinion, Wesley affirmed that such a transformation was possible before death. It was an entirely reasonable expectation that each believer should enter and enjoy that kind of Christian life here on this earth. This is what being a Christian is really about. *The Character of a Methodist* referred to above is

---

[5] John Wesley The Plain Account of Christian Perfection Epworth 1960. 44

shot through with scripture and makes it very plain that this kind of life is what God expects, requires and enables for each believer here and now.

Having tried to establish the progress of Wesley's thought and argument, we now need to examine his definition of Christian Perfection.

How Did Wesley Define Christian Perfection ?

Wesley's definition of Christian Perfection is simply the New Testament understanding of the Christian life as it ought to be lived. As Colin Williams states,
> It is only in the context of the total expression of the Christian life represented in Wesley's theology that his doctrine of perfection can be understood, for perfection is simply the climax of the limitless faith in God's grace that shines through every part of his theology. It is here that his theology comes to a focus.[6]

Wesley always defined perfection as the fulfilment of the Great Commandment
> The loving the Lord our God with all our heart, mind, soul and strength; and the loving our neighbour, every man, as our own souls. Such fulfilment 'implies that no wrong temper, none contrary to love, remains in the soul, and that all the thoughts, words and actions are governed by pure love'. In *The Scripture way of Salvation* he says, 'It is love excluding sin, love filling the heart, taking up the whole capacity of the soul.'[7]

That is the heart of the matter, yet it is not the whole matter. In his sermon 'On Perfection' Wesley gives us several features of this sanctification. He lists them in his own characteristic style
> 1. To love God with all one's heart and one's neighbour as oneself
> 2. To have the mind that is in Christ,
> 3. To bear the fruit of the Spirit (in accordance with Gal.5)
> 4. The restoration of the image of God in the soul of man, a recovery of man to the moral image of God, which consists of 'righteousness and true holiness'.
> 5. Inward and outward righteousness, 'holiness of life issuing from holiness of heart.
> 6. God's sanctifying of the person in spirit, soul and body.
> 7. The person's own perfect consecration to God.
> 8. A continuous presentation through Jesus of the individual's thoughts, words and actions as a sacrifice to God of praise and thanksgiving.
> 9. Salvation from all sin.

Much of Wesley's writing, teaching and preaching on the subject was not only to inform those seeking after holiness, but also to confound his many critics. They had serious problems with this doctrine, not least with the language which Wesley and his followers used. It is to a consideration of these criticisms which we must now turn.

---

[6] Colin Williams <u>John Wesley's Theology Today</u> New York. Abingdon 1960. 167/8

[7] William M Greathouse <u>John Wesley's Theology of Christian Perfection</u> Ilkeston. Moorley's. 4

Linguistic Problems

Perfection - Common usage

The word 'perfect' is an absolute word. By definition it rules out improvement. If improvement of a state or condition is possible the former state was, by definition, imperfect. Nor do some other phrases used to describe Christian Perfection help us. 'Entire sanctification' is no better. If one is 'entirely' sanctified the implication is that such a person could not be sanctified any more. Maybe these were some of the reasons that Wesley came to prefer the term 'Perfect Love' as a more appropriate description of the doctrine. Even so, Sangster asserts[8] that Wesley used the term 'Perfection' more than he realised. It was the title of his major apology on the subject and caused much difficulty for himself and his supporters, whilst providing ammunition for his critics.

To those not accustomed to his writings Wesley's clear and precise logic breaks down at this point. He uses the word 'perfection' and then warns his readers about the danger of setting the standard too high![9] We might well argue that if the standard was not as high as it could possibly be it would not be perfection as that word is commonly understood. The question then arises, 'Why did Wesley choose to use such a word ?' His answer is that it is scriptural.

Biblical words

The Authorised Version uses the word 'perfect' to translate the Greek *teleios*. Wesley used 'perfect' because it was Biblical, but if we are to understand what Wesley meant by it we must try and understand what the original Greek meant to those who wrote the New Testament. William Greathouse is right in affirming that it has a rich and varied meaning.[10] 'Whole', 'mature', 'without blemish' and 'full-grown' are all appropriate translations, depending on the context in which the word is used. Yet each translation must convey the central idea which lies behind *teleios* - the concept of a person or thing being all that they were intended to be. Once we have grasped this we are beginning to understand Wesley's concept. When he spoke of Christian Perfection he was referring to each Christian being all that a loving God intended them to be.

Thus, Wesley could argue that it was, in fact, possible to set the standard too high, presumably by expecting a person to be more than they were made or intended to be ay that point in their Christian journey. He makes the matter clear,

> ...your idea may go beyond, or at least beside, the scriptural account. It may include more than the Bible includes therein, or, however, something which that does not include. Scripture perfection is pure love, filling the heart, and governing all the words and action. [for that is what God intends] If your idea includes anything else, it is not scriptural; and then, no wonder that a scripturally perfect Christian does not come up to it.[11]

From the point of view of the one who has no knowledge of the seriousness with which Wesley treated the New Testament his view of perfection can be seen as a

---

[8] W.E. Sangster. The Path to Perfection. Hodder & Stoughton. 1943. 78
[9] Plain Account 46
[10] William Greathouse John Wesley's Theology of Christian Perfection Moorley's 1989. 5
[11] Plain Account 50, brackets mine

contradiction in terms, for it is not absolute perfection, but related to God's purpose and intention for each believer. It is to this 'limited' nature of perfection which we must now turn our attention.

'Limited' Perfection

Wesley's definition of sin.

Wesley defines sin, 'properly so called', as voluntary transgression of a known law. He allows that it is possible to involuntarily transgress a law, known or unknown, but he would not call this sin. Indeed, he argues the point conclusively from scripture. Yet he allows that because such involuntary transgressions do not conform to God's perfect and objective will for His creation, they still need the benefits of Christ's atoning blood. He has, consequently, no patience with those who, claiming perfection, refuse to seek God's forgiveness. If we were to try and understand this using concepts other than Wesley's we may find it helpful to speak of sins of omission and sins of commission. For Wesley sin was sin of commission. What we term sins of omission, the breaking of God's law when we did not know such a law existed, Wesley would not have termed sin, although he would allow that it needed the cleansing of Christ's atoning blood. For Wesley sin, 'properly so called' must involve the will.

We have a clue to his reason for restricting his definition of sin in this way in *The Plain Account*. He seeks to distinguish between sins (properly so called) and those mistakes or infirmities which he would not call sins but which others do. In stressing the importance of maintaining the distinction he says,

> I am much afraid, if we should allow any sins to be consistent with perfection, few would confine the idea to those defects concerning which only the assertion could be true.[12]

It is important, for Wesley, to assert that no sin is consistent with perfection, lest in allowing some 'so called sins' the list of sins so allowed should develop in an unscriptural way.

What Perfection is not

Wesley is at pains to point out that a 'perfect' Christian is still liable to make mistakes. Sometimes these will be errors of judgement which will result in mistakes in practice. Nor does he see that limitations of intellect or skill are inconsistent with perfection. As we have already stated involuntary transgression is also entirely consistent with the perfect Christian's life. He stresses the point,

> I believe there is no such perfection in this life as excludes these involuntary transgressions, which I apprehend to be naturally consequent on the ignorance and mistakes inseparable from mortality.[13]

The very essence of Christian Perfection is the nature of inward religion. It concerns motive, desire and intent. Wesley would assert that it is possible, by God's grace to live a life in which sin, as he defines it, has no place. We are still fallible, and in a sense part of a fallen creation, yet because God looks at the heart and sees what

---
[12] Plain Account 45
[13] Plain Account 45

others never see perfection is possible. Further, our very nature is transformed. Inbred sin is removed so that, even though we continue to be part of a fallen creation, our only desire is to do His will.

The point is well illustrated by remembering that when Charles Wesley originally wrote the hymn 'Love Divine, all loves excelling' he included a line,

> 'take from us the power of sinning'

It was John Fletcher, Vicar of Madeley, who corrected it to read

> 'take from us the bent to sinning'

Most modern hymn books amend it to

> 'take from us the love of sinning'

but the Methodist Hymn Book and Hymns and Psalms, just to be on the safe side, omits the verse altogether!

As one has succinctly put it the Christian is not unable to sin, but always able not to sin. Wesley would add, 'nor does he want to', for his inner nature has been transformed by the grace of God.

The Contrast with Justification

Through his doctrine of Christian Perfection Wesley holds out the possibility for every Christian to enter a new dimension in Christian living. It consists of a life lived for God and by His power. It is distinct from, and subsequent to, justification. The contrast needs to be clearly understood. When we become Christians we are justified. The guilt of sin is dealt with, but through sanctification the disease of sin is cured. When we become Christians we enter a new relationship with God in which, even though we are sinners we are counted righteous because of Christ. Here we are made righteous through the ministry of the Holy Spirit. When we become Christians we are restored to God's favour, here we are restored to God's image. This is not just about a change in our status, but a change in our nature. Justification marks something done for us, but sanctification concerns something done in us. Even though Wesley understood that the work of sanctification begins when we become Christians he proclaimed a deeper work of grace, distinct from and subsequent to justification, the entrance into a life of Perfect Love.

Such a life is entered into by simple faith and Wesley expects it as an instantaneous experience. However, it does not come by accident. Wesley makes it clear that each believer must go through a convicting work, as prior to justification, but at a deeper level. Earnest desire is the key which unlocks the door into a life of Perfect Love. And he is quite sure that those who have entered such a life know that they have so entered.

> 'None therefore ought to believe that the work is done, until there is added the testimony of the Spirit witnessing his entire sanctification as clearly as his justification.'[14]

During the revival which accompanied Wesley's ministry many bore testimony to the experience. They obviously impressed him very deeply. He includes the testimony of Jane Cooper in *Plain Account* (63ff) yet we must remember that he is speaking, not of the emotional experience of a moment, but rather a new way of Christian living which proved its validity in the lives of many people over many years. In 1766

---
[14] Plain Account 52

during the Otley Revival many people professed that they had entered into Christian Perfection. This awakening quickly spread to other Methodist societies and John Wesley closely investigated the phenomena. Year later he wrote,

> Here began that glorious work of sanctification, which had been nearly at a stand for twenty years. But from time to time it spread, first through various parts of Yorkshire, afterwards in London, then through most parts of England; next through Dublin. Limerick and all the south and west of Ireland. And wherever the work of sanctification increased, the whole work of God increased in all its branches.[15]

Wesley went to meet and interview many of those who had entered into blessing. The evidence of their changed lives added to his conviction concerning the truth of this doctrine. In London he 'carefully examined' six hundred and fifty two such people, of whom he writes,

> And every one of these...has declared that his deliverance from sin was instantaneous, that the change was wrought in a moment. Had half of these, or one third, or one in twenty, declared that it was gradually wrought in them, I should have believed this, with regard to them, and thought that some were gradually sanctified and some instantaneously. But as I have not found, in so long a space of time, a single person speaking thus; as all who believe they are sanctified, declared with one voice, that the change was wrought in a moment, I cannot but believe that sanctification is commonly, if not always, an instantaneous work.[16]

Facets of Perfection

People are often confused by some of the terms used to describe Christian Perfection. I find it helpful to think of them as facets on a jewel which, when turned in the light of God's love, reveal a series of distinct but complementary truths, each one a brilliant insight into God's heart for each believer. Just as there are a variety of ways of describing justification which are complementary, not contradictory, so there are a variety of ways of describing perfection. We shall examine some of them.

Purity of Heart

> *Give me a new, a perfect heart,*
> *From doubt and fear and sorrow free,*
> *The mind which was in Christ impart,*
> *And let my spirit cleave to Thee.*

Wesley was convinced that God could do more with sin than forgive it. He looked for and proclaimed a deeper, more profound, work of grace which involved not just the forgiveness of sin committed but a change in the nature of the believer. His perception of the Christian life was one in which the believer did not commit sin, as Wesley defined it, simply because he no longer wanted to. His very nature and inner desire had been changed. Now his sole desire was to do his Master's will.

---

[15] John Wesley Works 13:350
[16] John Wesley Works 3:178

This raises the question as to whether sin can ever be entirely eradicated from the human soul. This is terminology which Wesley himself would not have used but he did speak of the removal of 'inbred' sin, or the 'bent to sinning'. If this is what people mean by eradication, then clearly this is where Wesley stands. One suspects, however, that those who use 'eradication' terminology want to go father than Wesley would have found comfortable.

Another way of addressing this issue is to view it objectively and subjectively. Objectively i.e. from God's point of view, there may remain sin in the believers heart, but it will be sin of which the believer is unaware. Subjectively, on the other hand, all sin of which he is aware has been removed and his heart is as clean as he is aware it can be. Bringing these two perspectives together helps us to understand how Wesley perceives perfection as a process of sanctification. Each moment the believer is as clean as he can be in that moment, but as he becomes aware of sin at a level hitherto unrealised, he comes to Christ in repentance and faith and receives a deeper cleaning than he has hitherto known,

> *Teach me as my soul can bear,*
> *The depth of inbred sin,*
> *All the unbelief declare,*
> *The pride that lurks within.*
> *Take me, whom Thyself has bought,*
> *Bring into captivity,*
> *Every high, aspiring thought,*
> *Which would not stoop to Thee.*

This is essentially inner religion, purity of heart at its finest. Wesley is supremely concerned about the conscience, the motive and the desire. For him a perfect Christian is one who can come to a Holy God without a sense of shame.

Christian Maturity

> *Thy nature gracious Lord impart,*
> *Come quickly from above,*
> *Write Thy new Name upon my heart,*
> *Thy new, best Name of Love*

William Greathouse stresses this aspect of Wesley's doctrine as he draws our attention to *teleios* as a word used to describe that which is fulfilling the purpose for which it was intended. In that sense Wesley believes that God's purposes can be fulfilled in every believer.

> For him [Wesley] the perfect Christian is not one who is flawless or infallible but one who is 'conformed to the end' of his existence i.e. to love God supremely and his fellow man as his own soul.[17]

This ability, to love God and man perfectly, is a consequence of Christ dwelling within the life of the perfect Christian. Indeed, Christ within has become the mainspring of his life. The transformation of character which the perfect Christian

---

[17] William Greathouse John Wesley's Theology of Christian Perfection 4

exhibits is because his character has become the character of Christ. Speaking of Paul's words 'I am crucified with Christ; nevertheless I live; yet not I, but Christ liveth in me' and describing the life of the perfect Christian, Wesley says,

> He is purified from pride; for Christ was lowly in heart. He is pure from desire and self-will: for Christ desired only to do the will of His Father. And he is pure from anger, in the common sense of that word; for Christ was meek and gentle.[18]

R.L Maddox puts it another way,

> Wesley was convinced that the Christian life did not have to remain a life of continual struggle. He believed that both Scripture and Christian tradition attested that God's loving grace can transform our lives to the point where our own love for God and others becomes a 'natural' response. Christians can aspire to take on the disposition of Christ, and live out that disposition within the constraints of our human infirmities. To deny that possibility would be to deny the sufficiency of God's empowering grace - to make the power of sin greater than that of grace.[19]

It is Wesley's deep conviction that God's purpose is to make us like Jesus. Through his doctrine of Christian perfection he places that ideal within the reach of any who have the faith to claim God's promises.

Complete Devotion

> *Now let me gain perfection's height,*
> *Now let me into nothing fall,*
> *By less than nothing in Thy sight,*
> *And feel that Christ is all in all.*

From his days at Oxford Wesley had been consumed by a passion for God. He was convinced that man's first duty was to be entirely devoted to God. The influence of the Moravians reaching its climax in the Aldersgate experience introduced him to the glorious possibility of heart religion. It was entirely natural that the religion which he proclaimed throughout his ministry was one in which each believer loved God with his entire being. In *The Character of a Methodist*, first issued in 1742, he wrote,

> A Methodist is one who loves the Lord his God with all his heart, with all his soul, with all his mind, and with all his strength. God is the joy of his heart, and the desire of his soul, which is continually crying "Whom have I in heaven but Thee? and there is none upon earth whom I desire beside Thee." My God and my all![20]

Whilst there was no doubt in his mind concerning this dimension of heart religion, and whilst the Aldersgate experience helped him to make such a religion his own; it was his developing understanding of Christian Perfection which brought this goal within range for every Christian. He saw justification as man claiming his inheritance in the grace of God. In contrast Christian Perfection was the result of man's total self-offering to God in thankfulness for His gift in Christ. Wesley thus established the relationship between consecration and holiness, a relationship which was to prove

---

[18] Plain Account 20
[19] R.L Maddox Responsible Grace Nashville. Kingswood. 1994 188
[20] Plain Account 11

crucial in the holiness movements which followed the Methodist revival. Writing of this consecrated life, the life of the perfect Christian, Wesley wrote in 1777

> In one view, it is purity of intention, dedicating all the life to God. It is the giving to God all our hearts: it is one desire and design ruling all our tempers. It is devoting, not a part, but all our soul, body and substance to God.[21]

Commenting on the centrality of this devotion in the life of the perfect Christian, Rupert Davies writes,

> Christian Perfection is, above all, loving God with all our heart and soul and mind and strength, and our neighbour as ourselves; and 'loving' is here to be construed in no formal or abstract sense, but in the deepest, most intimate, most personal, most far-reaching way. The best possible description of it, therefore, is Perfect Love.[22]

Nor should we assume that Wesley's concept primarily concerned a momentous crisis experience which may be fulfilling for the moment but of little lasting worth. Whilst experience convinced him that such an experience was at least likely in the searching heart, the value lay not in the experience alone, but in the life of constant consecration to which the experience was simply the doorway. When identifying the hall-marks of Christian Perfection in the believer's life Newton Flew identifies the first in this way 'The goal is uninterrupted communion with God'[23]

Many have sought to identify the moment when Wesley himself knew the experience of entering such a life. Some have pointed to the Love Feast held on New Years Eve 1739. Yet the most likely moment seems to be December 24th 1744 when, in his Journal, he writes

> In the evening I found such light and strength as I never remember to have had before. I saw every thought as well as every action or word, just as it was rising in my heart; and whether it was right before God, or tainted with pride or selfishness. I never knew before (I mean not as at this time) what it was 'to be still before God'
>
> *Tuesday 25th* I walked by the grace of God in the same spirit; and about eight, being with two or three that believed in Jesus, I felt such an awe and tender sense of the presence of God as greatly confirmed me therein: so that God was before me all the day long. I sought and found Him in every place; and could truly say, when I lay down at night, 'Now I have *lived* a day'.[24]

Whether this experience was his entry into Christian Perfection we cannot know. Yet we can say with some certainty that it helped shape his thinking on the subject. From his own experience he knew that uninterrupted communion with God was possible and in proclaiming Scriptural Holiness throughout the land he was offering that same dimension in Christian living to all who would receive it.

---

[21] Plain Account 109
[22] R. Davies A History of the Methodist Church in Great Britain. Vol. 1 London. Epworth 1965. 171.
[23] N Flew. The Idea of Perfection London. Oxford University Press. 1934. 329
[24] quoted by N. Flew The Idea of Perfection 329

Love Excluding Sin

> *Love Divine, all loves excelling,*
> *Joy of heaven, to earth come down,*
> *Fix in us Thy humble dwelling,*
> *All Thy faithful mercies crown.*
> *Jesu' Thou art all compassion,*
> *Pure unbounded love Thou art,*
> *Visit us with Thy salvation,*
> *Enter every trembling heart*

Wesley, and those who embrace his theology of Christian Perfection, have frequently been criticised for using absolute words - entire, perfect, filled, complete, all. One can understand the criticism, yet one can also understand why such words are necessary. Wesley's understanding was that when the human heart was filled with the love of Christ there was no room left for anything else. If the believer is completely devoted to God every other claim on his affections pales into insignificance. As Wesley himself put it,

> Entire Sanctification, or Christian Perfection, is neither more nor less than pure love - love expelling sin and governing both the heart and life of a child of God.[25]

Sangster, when commenting on the immense love of God invading the believer's heart, says,

> In the sense which he had defined sin, this love expelled sin from the heart and life of those who received it. They did not commit sin. Sometimes, he says, they *cannot* commit sin, but, in the great majority of instances in which he uses this expression, he is, of course, not denying their capacity but only stressing the steadiness of a will "uniformly devoted to God".[26]

Emphasising this aspect of Christian Perfection, Wesley says,

> We feel the love of God shed abroad in our heart by the Holy Ghost which is given unto us; producing love to all mankind, and more especially to the children of God; expelling the love of the world, the love of pleasure, of ease, of honour, of money, together with pride, anger, self-will, and every other evil temper; in a word changing the earthly, sensual, devilish mind, into 'the mind which was in Christ Jesus'[27]

Again Wesley says

> ...as long as love takes up the whole heart, what room is there for sin therein?[28]

---

[25] Letters, 3.168 quoted by W.E Sangster The Path to Perfection 77
[26] W.E Sangster The Path to Perfection 80
[27] Seromn 'The Scripture Way of Salvation' - Standard Sermons 2. 446
[28] Ths Standard Sermons of John Wesley ed. Sugden 2. 457

Perfect Love

O that I now from sin released,
Thy word may to the utmost prove
Enter into the promised rest,
The Caanan of Thy perfect love

Wesley's basic conviction was that God's love is for all. When preparing for ordination in 1725 he read again the Thirty-Nine Articles of the Church of England. He was deeply troubled by the article dealing with predestination. Interestingly it was to his mother, Susanna, that he turned for guidance. In her reply[29] she pointed out that God's predestination was determined by his foreknowledge (Rom 8:29). She also commented that the doctrine of predestination, as understood by some Calvinists, was shocking. John entirely agreed. Preaching on 'Free Grace' he says,

> Here I fix my foot. On this I join issue with every asserter of it. You represent God as worse than the devil - more false, more cruel, more unjust.[30]

God's love for all is fundamental and it is supremely demonstrated in a cross. Following the Aldersgate experience all his doctrines were atonement centred. The Moravian influence had proved decisive in convincing him that saving faith was not assent to a proposition, but personal trust in the atoning death of Christ. Before long he and his brother were singing about 'Amazing love' for they had known, not just about the love of God, they had known it 'shed abroad in their hearts'. The love which they felt for God and others was but a reflection of God's love for them. This became the 'new law written on their hearts'. Yet that did not set them free from moral obligation. Anyone who knows anything about the controversies with the antinomians understands how important morality was to Wesley. Yet now the motive was different. Christian morality was not about keeping an exterior imposed law, but about expressing our new and supernatural love for God and neighbour; yet in the very expressing of that love the divine law is fulfilled.

The life of holiness is a life where this great love of God controls all our thoughts, words and actions. Randy Maddox. puts it succinctly. Speaking about Wesley's understanding of Christian Perfection as Perfect Love he says,

> Thus, when he wanted to be more specific he would define Christian Perfection as 'the humble, gentle, patient love of God, and our neighbour, ruling our tempers, words and actions.' It is important to note that love is not only said to be present, it is *ruling*. God's love is shed abroad in the lives of all Christians, awakening their responsive love for God and others. But this love is weak, sporadic, and offset by contrary affections in new believers. In the lives of the entirely sanctified Wesley maintained that it rules 'to the point that there is no mixture of any contrary affection - all is peace and harmony'.[31]

At the heart of Wesley's message lay the deep conviction that human nature could be changed. The grace of God, revealed in Jesus, poured into believing hearts

---

[29] recorded in Abingdon *Works* vol. 25
[30] The Works of John Wesley Abingdon. 1987 3:556
[31] Randy Maddox Responsible Grace Nashville. Kingswood. 1994. 187

through the Holy Spirit, could do for individual people what they could never do for themselves. They could become new people, not in theory, but in fact.

The essence of Entire Sanctification is that at long last these ingrained faults of human nature, even redeemed human nature, are purged away. But they are not just purged away; they are superseded, overwhelmed, by positive qualities of humility, tenderness, compassion, love. There is no inadequacy about an ideal such as this. Rather it seems unattainable to poor, weak mortals such as ourselves - and is, except by the power of the Holy Spirit.[32]

The Way In

Wesley was, supremely, a man with a mission. He sets forth the 'high plateau' of Christian Perfection, not as academic theology, but because he wants every Christian to enter this dimension of Christian living; to be a 'New Testament Christian'. He was anxious not only in his own preaching, but in the guidance which he gave to his preachers, to set out the steps which a believer might expect to take in order to enter this life. We shall try and state them plainly.

We are constrained to seek the things of God by God's prevenient grace at work within us.

Conviction of sin, which is part of this work, leads to repentance and faith.

By grace, through faith, we are put in a new relationship with God, not through any merit of our own, but through the merit of Christ's atoning death. We are justified by faith. Our sin is forgiven.

At the same time we are born again, made new people in Christ. An inner change takes place. Sanctification begins.

Wesley expects that, following justification, each believer will have a growing awareness, not of his sin, but of his sinfulness. A conviction regarding this sinfulness, parallel to the conviction prior to justification, will grip his soul.

By placing his faith in Christ, as he did at justification, the believer can know his sinful nature dealt with. He is entirely renewed within. His heart is completely cleansed from sin and filled with the love of God.

This crisis moment is the doorway to a life of holiness in which there is a steady growth in grace and love.

Christian Perfection, so entered and enjoyed, ought not to be seen as a *state* of sanctification, if that suggests that a permanent achievement can be secured in a moment of Christian experience. The experience marks not the destination, but the beginning, or at least a mile-post, on the journey. It is the point of entry into a life which is lived in moment-by-moment consecration. Writing to John Mason he

---

[32] Rupert Davies. ;A History of the Methodist Church in Great Britain vol. 1 173

advises him to 'press all the believers to go on to perfection and to expect deliverance from sin every moment'[33]

The Holy Spirit bears witness with the perfected Christian that the change had been wrought in his life.

There is always the possibility of regression if constant communion, for which the means of grace are provided, is not maintained.

Conclusion

I guess that many of us here tonight have some reservations about Christian Perfection as Wesley understood and proclaimed it. We are maybe conscious of the contrast between the days of revival in which he ministered and the days of decline in which we live. He travelled throughout the Kingdom by horse at the dawn of the industrial revolution. Today we live in a world of instant communication on the threshold of a new millennium.

Yet I believe that human beings are essentially the same and, more importantly, God's love and power is essentially the same. I may choose to state Wesley's theology differently, but I believe that he was right.

I believe, with Wesley, that it was for the proclamation of scriptural holiness that God raised up the Methodist people. If ever there was a doctrine which needed to be grasped, restated and proclaimed today it is this doctrine. I long for the day when we as a church will begin to take scriptural holiness seriously again. Too often we have lost the relationship between the religious and the moral dimension of faith. Here they are united. Too often we have seen holiness as the preserve of the few. Here it is placed within reach of every believer. Too often we have divorced spirituality and evangelism. Here they are united. Too often we have polarised theology and experience. Here the one lead to, and then enables the other.

I am not naive enough to believe that a new stress on holiness would bring an instant answer to all our problems; but I am convinced that its restatement in a language which ordinary people today can understand would bring a new vitality to the Methodist people. To proclaim this is our great privilege. To ignore or remain silent about it is to deny the very purpose for which God raised up the people called Methodists.

---

[33] W.E Sangster The Path to Perfection 86

Bibliography

R. Davies A History of the Methodist Church in Great Britain. Vol. 1 London. Epworth 1965.

M.E Dieter Five Views on Sanctification Grand Rapids. Zondervan 1987

N Flew. The Idea of Perfection London. Oxford University Press. 1934.

William M Greathouse John Wesley's Theology of Christian Perfection Ilkeston. Moorley's.

J.M. Gordon Evangelical Spirituality London. S.P.C.K. 1991

R.L Maddox Responsible Grace Nashville. Kingswood. 1994

A.C. Outler John Wesley New York. O.U.P. 1964

A.C. Outler The Works of John Wesley Nashville. Abingdon. 1987

J.I Packer. Keep in Step with the Spirit Leicester. Inter-Varsity Press. 1988

W.E. Sangster The Path to Perfection London, Hodder & Stoughton. 1943.

J. Telford.(ed.) The Letters of John Wesley London. Epworth. 1931

G.A Turner. The Vision which Transforms Kansas City. Beacon Hill Press. 1964.

J. Wesley. A Plain Account of Christian Perfection London. Epworth Press 1960

J Wesley. The Standard Sermons of John Wesley London. Epworth. 1968

Colin Williams John Wesley's Theology Today New York. Abingdon 1960.

A.S. Wood The Burning Heart Exeter Paternoster. 1967

M.B. Wynkoop A Theology of Love Kansas City. Beacon Hill. 1972

A movement of Methodists committed to prayer for revival and witness to the evangelical faith.

The aims of the movement are...

- The promotion of the renewal and revival of the work, worship, and witness of the Church, particularly within Methodism, through prayer and in the power of the Holy Spirit.
- The encouragement of prayer for revival at a personal level, and in the church at home and overseas.
- The furtherance of informed theological discussion in the Church.
- The furtherance of thinking and action on ethical and social issues in a responsible and compassionate way, based on the belief that the righteous will of God must be expressed in the life of Society.
- The promotion of joint action with evangelical Christians in all denominations of the Church in local and national events.
- The promotion of mature Christian spirituality in the lives of all members of the Church.

Our basis of faith is that of the Evangelical Alliance, with a specific commitment to the Methodist understanding of salvation, as set out in the FOUR ALLS.
- All people need to be saved
- All people can be saved
- All people can know themselves to be saved
- All people can be saved to the uttermost

Membership of HEADWAY is open to any member of the Methodist Church who is in sympathy with the aims and basis of the movement. Associate membership is open to those who are not members of the Methodist Church. HEADWAY is a Registered Charity No. 298087.

Further information from the Membership Secretary:

        Mr Neil Baldock
        1 Garraways
        Woodshaw
        Wootton Bassett
        Swindon
        Wilts SN4 8LT